BOOTS SHOES

1032.

Real Horse-shoe pitching in Kan.

Copyright 1909 by Martin Post Card Co.

LARGER THAN LIFE

THE AMERICAN TALL-TALE POSTCARD, 1905-1915

CYNTHIA ELYCE RUBIN

AND

MORGAN WILLIAMS

ABBEVILLE PRESS ❧ PUBLISHERS ❧ NEW YORK

Editor: Walton Rawls
Designer: Julie Rauer
Copy Chief: Robin James
Production Supervisor: Hope Koturo

Library of Congress Cataloging-in-Publication Data

Rubin, Cynthia Elyce.
Larger than life : the American tall-tale postcard, 1905–1915 /
Cynthia Elyce Rubin and Morgan Williams.
p. cm.
Includes bibliographical references.
ISBN 1-55859-014-5
1. Postcards—United States.   2. Tall tales in art.   I. Williams,
Morgan.   II. Title.
NC1878.7.U6R8   1990
741.6′83′097309041—dc20   89-77978
                                                             CIP

We are grateful to the following institutions for permission to reproduce items in
their collections: Iowa State Historical Department, Des Moines, Iowa (page 61);
Kansas State Historical Society, Topeka, Kansas (page 73); New-York Historical
Society, New York City (pages 7, 102); New York State Historical Association,
Cooperstown, New York (pages 12, 13); Waupun Historical Society, Waupun,
Wisconsin (page 108). Unless otherwise indicated, all cards reproduced are from
the collection of E. Morgan Williams.

CONTENTS

LARGER
THAN LIFE

Andy Warhol seems to have said it all: everyone has his fifteen minutes of fame. Stretching that bit of wisdom to include the myriad fads and fancies of our lifetime—among them the hoola hoop, the pet rock, and, of course, the tall-tale photographic postcard—one might easily acknowledge that history has validated Warhol's thesis.

When around the turn of the century the newly settled Midwest was suddenly hit with violent climatic change—drought, flood, hail, blizzard, and even swarms of grasshoppers—something exceptional was called for to help the farmers cope. Reality had given the lie to stories and advertisements that lured people to a land said to be so fertile at harvest time that a man could get lost in his own luxuriant fields. Not about to admit to anyone their growing disappointment with their new home, these settlers were more likely to exaggerate a bit down at the county seat when telling about their crops. Though privately these farmers wondered why grasshoppers came a second time when there was nothing left for them to ravage, they never failed to boast in cards and letters to family and friends back East of their record yields. This way of coping led directly to the short-lived comic phenomenon that prompted this book—a visual counterpart to the frontier tall tale—and made a profound impression on the minds of its generation. To some extent that impact continues on as a valuable source of insight into the emergence of modern America.

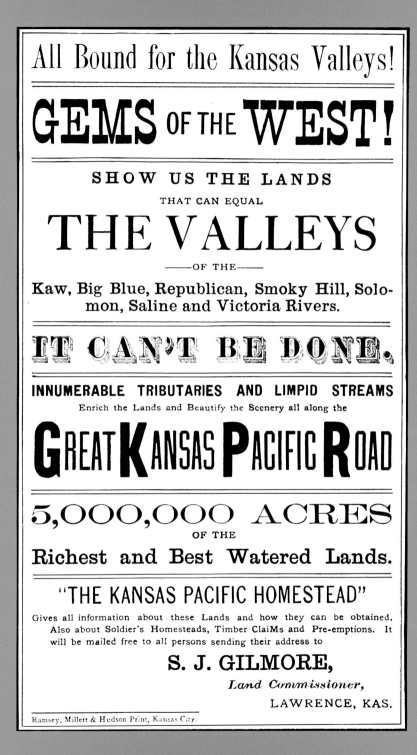

All Bound for the Kansas Valleys!

GEMS OF THE WEST!

SHOW US THE LANDS

THAT CAN EQUAL

THE VALLEYS

—— OF THE ——

Kaw, Big Blue, Republican, Smoky Hill, Solomon, Saline and Victoria Rivers.

IT CAN'T BE DONE.

INNUMERABLE TRIBUTARIES AND LIMPID STREAMS

Enrich the Lands and Beautify the Scenery all along the

GREAT KANSAS PACIFIC ROAD

5,000,000 ACRES

OF THE

Richest and Best Watered Lands.

"THE KANSAS PACIFIC HOMESTEAD"

Gives all information about these Lands and how they can be obtained. Also about Soldier's Homesteads, Timber ClaiMs and Pre-emptions. It will be mailed free to all persons sending their address to

S. J. GILMORE,

Land Commissioner,

LAWRENCE, KAS.

Ramsey, Millett & Hudson Print, Kansas City.

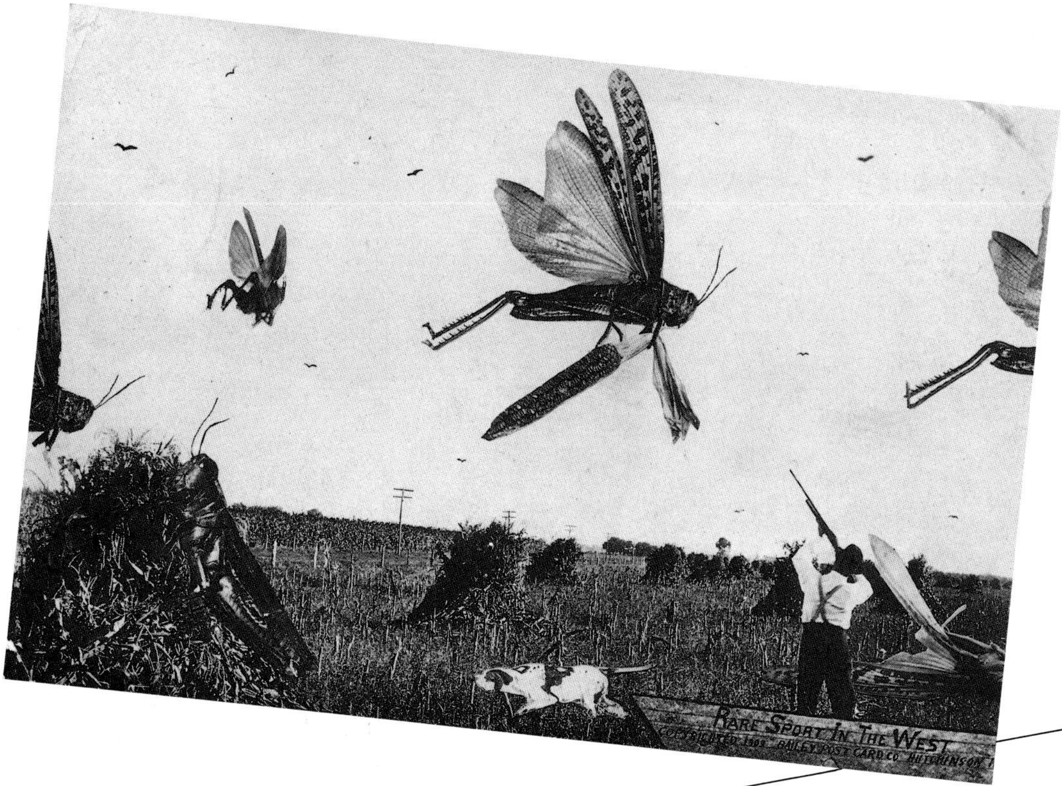

RARE SPORT IN THE WEST
COPYRIGHTED 1908 BAILEY POST CARD CO. HUTCHINSON

UNITED STATES OF AMERICA
1706 FRANKLIN 1790
1
1
POSTAGE
ONE CENT

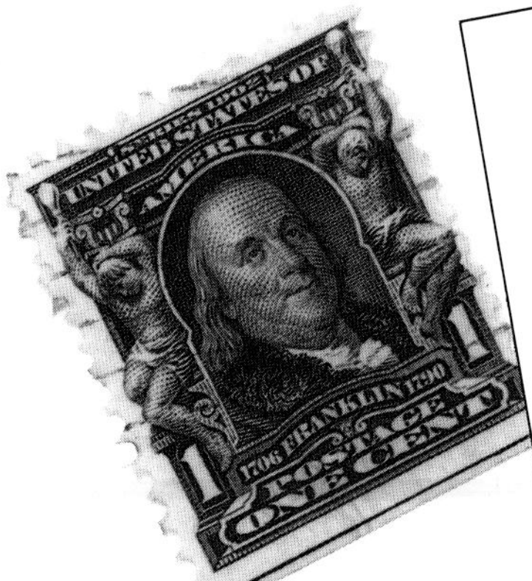

1908

Dear Friend:— As this is such a marvelous land of plenty I have decided to remain in Kansas. I drove out into the country the other day and seeing a big orchard, I asked the farmer for an apple, when he got it for me he had to bring it in a wheelbarrow. Cornstalks are so big they're cutting them up into railroad ties; and they grow so fast that if a man plants corn on Saturday night he has to have a force of lumbermen on hand Monday morning to chop it down and get the ears off. I saw one man at plowing, turn dirt on a street-car ticket and the next minute a trolley car whized off and scared his team to death. I'd plant a dollar but for the danger of getting a crop of eagles.

Yours in divine truthfulness.

THE BIG RED APPLE
ON U. S. HIGHWAY 36
Largest Apple Ever Grown
30 feet high   100 feet in circumference
Eight miles west of St. Joseph, Mo. near Wathena, Kan.
Pat. App. For   See front of card

For this ultimate example of American visual hyperbole to have occurred at all, timing had to be exactly right—and so it was, a precise confluence of certain factors with the incredible vastness of the frontier and its extraordinary variety of natural disasters. American social history, the new technology of photography, and the American penchant for inventiveness unerringly combined with the urge to make an extra buck.

American reality has always been larger than life. We bear witness to the immensity of the Grand Canyon; to the vast treeless stretches of the Plains and the large expanse of the Dakota prairies; to high buildings always built higher and higher; to airplanes turned into airbuses; to roadside sculptures of the biggest fish, the biggest duck, and the biggest prairie chicken; to a water tower masquerading as a huge peach. Nothing seems exempt. Despite their scientific credulity, Americans love to adjust expressions of scale to their own version of reality.

In their travel accounts, early visitors to America often told of the settlers' love of exaggeration. Travelers recalled hearing incredible tales swapped on stagecoaches, steamboats, and around campfires, and most stories were funny. They described the antics of huge animals, giant insects, eccentric hunters, and fish that got away in rivers too thick to drink and too thin to plow. Others dealt with hard times, the land's fertility, and the weather, which "if there weren't bad weather, there wouldn't be no weather at all!"

According to Carolyn Brown, author of *The Tall Tale*, while this special kind of drollery flourished on steamboats and in

ATCHISON, KANSAS

1906

"Driven from Home in the year of the TERRIBLE CROPS IN KANSAS."

Whatever was planted has grown so beyond control that houses are wrecked, fences demolished, buildings pushed aside, traffic ways obstructed; and all plans for harvesting and moving the produce seem to be unavailing.

From the Kansas City Times.

barrooms, it also blossomed forth in popular formats for written humor, notably in local newspaper stories. A cub reporter from Winsted, Connecticut, Louis T. Stone, soon learned that if he couldn't sell routine stories to the big-city papers, he could succeed by manipulating the news. His big year was 1895, and the story was an account of a wild man at large in the Connecticut woods. Stone followed up with an article about a tree on which baked apples grew, a cow that gave burning milk after grazing in a horseradish patch, and a man who painted a spider on his bald head to keep the flies away. Because of these concoctions, Stone became known as the "Winsted Liar," and when he died in 1933, the town bridge over Sucker Brook was dedicated to his memory.

There were predecessors. Joseph Mulholland, a traveling salesman from Pennsylvania, wrote under the pseudonym of Orange Blossom in the 1880s and '90s, mainly for the *Philadelphia Public Ledger*. Among his most interesting stories was one about a blazing meteor that fell in western Pennsylvania and set fire to a large portion of the country. Cleveland's *Plain Dealer* chronicled the activities of a Captain I. D. Howard of North Geneva, Ohio, who discovered a pet rattlesnake using a stick to rob his hens' nests and of increasing the daily output of Bessie, his cow, by feeding her Vitamin D breakfast food.

A contributing factor to belief in many of the newspaper tales was the prestige of the printed word. Despite frequent fulminations against the daily paper, ordinary readers derived from its pages most of their real knowledge of what was going on in the world. Likewise, people would later come to respect the radio as a trustworthy medium of information. Certainly, when people tune in the news, they do not ever imagine they will be duped. That situation would change somewhat as a result of a broadcast on October 30, 1938, when thousands of Americans from coast to coast panicked over a radio dramatization by Orson Welles of H. G. Wells's fantastic *War of the Worlds.* Shifting the locale from England to New Jersey and adopting radio news broadcast techniques, Welles convinced listeners that accounts of heat-ray-spurting Martians were as authentic as those of contemporary crises in Europe. Despite regular announcements that the program was a dramatization of an old novel, thousands of New York and New Jersey residents left their homes to seek refuge, and hospitals treated hundreds for shock. People got out their firearms and hastened to the outskirts of Princeton where rocketships full of octopuslike invaders were said to have landed.

More recently, Garrison Keillor re-

ported on "A Prairie Home Companion" the news from Lake Wobegon, a nonexistant place where "smart doesn't count for much." It was an unforgettable portrait of a small town where a hazy realm of fiction was always colliding with fact.

P. T. Barnum said over and over again that the public likes to be fooled. Many a tale intended to have only a fleeting effect has grown to huge proportions. In a land where measurements encourage blind faith, a giant hoax could easily flourish. Take the case of George Hull. Physically overwhelming at six feet with stooped shoulders and a ruddy complexion, Hull looked the very image of a villain. While on a visit to his sister in Ackley, Iowa, he became intrigued with a Biblical verse he heard quoted: "There were giants in the earth in those days" (Genesis 6:4). A confirmed atheist in a time of religious conviction, he was fascinated by the fact that people might actually believe in giants. Hull got a brainstorm.

Selling his cigar business, he moved to Iowa and obtained a block of gypsum 12 feet by 4 feet by 22 inches. He shipped it to Chicago and hired two sculptors to carve a stone giant. Because it looked too new upon completion, Hull experimented with various aging techniques. To simulate skin pores, he hammered away with hundreds of large darning needles set into a block of wood. To give a patina, he washed the sculpture with ink followed by a bath of sulphuric acid. Finally the giant was shipped circuitously to Cardiff, New York, and buried in an area known for rich deposits of fossils and ancient relics. Hull then quietly returned to cigar manufacturing and waited for an opportune moment.

THE GREAT
CARDIFF GIANT!

Discovered at Cardiff. Onondaga So. N. Y., is now on Exhibition in the

Geological Hall, Albany,

For a few days only.

HIS DIMENSIONS.

Length of Body,	10 feet. 4 1-2 inches.
Length of Head from Chin to Top of Head,	21 "
Length of Nose.	6 "
Across the Nostrils.	3 1-2 "
Width of Mouth,	5 "
Circumference of Neck,	37 "
Shoulders. from point to point.	3 feet. 1 1-2 "
Length of Right Arm.	4 feet. 9 1-2 "
Across the Wrist.	5 "
Across the Palm of Hand.	7 "
Length of Second Finger.	8 "
Around the Thighs.	6 feet. 3 1-2 "
Diameter of the Thigh.	13 "
Through the Calf of Leg.	9 1-2 "
Length of Foot.	21 "
Across the Ball of Foot.	8 "
Weight.	2990 pounds.

ALBANY November 29th. 1869.

He had done his best to insure success for his scheme; the rest of its unfolding would depend on a zealous public.

On October 16, 1869, according to plan, men were hired to dig a well where the giant had been buried. Voilà, a foot and then a body appeared. As curiosity seekers gathered around the excavation, the Cardiff Giant's career took hold. The next day, a tent was erected and an admission fee of 50 cents per person per quarter-hour's viewing was initiated. Arriving from all corners of New York and surrounding states, people came in droves. The locals were making money hand over fist, for the visitors had to eat, sleep, buy souvenirs, and be entertained. Barely a week after its first showing, Hull sold a three-quarters interest in the mammoth petrified man to a consortium of New York state's most upstanding citizens, thus further legitimizing the Giant's antiquity.

While on tour, the giant began to show signs of artificial manufacture, but suspicions about its age already had been mounting. Finally, the opinion of O. C. Marsh, a Yale paleontologist, left no doubt: "It is of very recent origin and a decided humbug."

Despite negative scientific testimony, the Giant experienced a very slow death. It traveled the carnival circuit for some time before hitting the skids; ultimately it ended up in a home in Des Moines, Iowa. In the late 1940s it was rediscovered as a piece of American folklore and moved to the Farmers' Museum in Cooperstown, New York, taking its place once again in the folk life of that state.

Of petrified men, there have been many. One of the most popular was that exhibited at the Chicago World's Columbian Exposition in 1893—the "Forest City Man" from somewhere in the Dakotas. It had been manufactured out of a human skeleton, buried, and then dug up by a friend of the maker. Another imitation was the "Pine River Man," discovered in 1876 and described in *Popular Science* as being "no Cardiff Giant, but a bona-fide 'creation of God.' " The "Colorado Man" was a most ambitious effort; with a four-inch tail and arms proportionally longer than its legs, it looked more like a monster than a man. When a traveling "geologist" discovered the body in its Rocky Mountain burial

"The Cardiff Giant— Hoisting the Statue from the Pit," after an original photograph by C. O. Gott. Courtesy New York State Historical Association, Cooperstown, New York.

place, P. T. Barnum just happened to be in the neighborhood. Despite an exposé by Yale's O. C. Marsh, the Colorado Man entertained Westerners for some time. It is doubtful, however, that its promoters ever gained much on their investment.

To some extent, capitalism is a big part of what it's all about. Paul Bunyan, mighty logger, whose tall-tale exploits were first published in an article by James MacGillivray in the Detroit *News Tribune* in 1910, was not a national folk figure until he was born with the help of obstetrician W. B. Laughead, a Minneapolis ad man and ex-lumberjack. Hired in 1914 to promote products for the Red River Lumber Company of Akeley, Minnesota, he attracted buyers and city folks to the Minnesota timberlands through his caricatures and stories.

When Bunyan's likeness was adopted as the Red River trademark, to stand "for the quality and service you have the right to expect from Paul Bunyan," supersalesman Laughead began to create an exemplification of the American spirit that re-

fuses to die. From Bangor, Maine, to Oregon, promoters now claim Paul Bunyan as a native son, but nowhere is he more a part of the local heritage than in Minnesota Lake country. Tiny Akeley, home of about 500 people, today displays Paul's oversize wooden cradle and his biggest statue (to date), a 33-foot fiberglass colossus erected near Frank's supermarket.

Scores of tall tales about Bunyan's lesser-known counterparts have cropped up all over the country: Tony Beaver, denizen of southern forests; Pecos Bill, creator of Great Salt Lake; Dave Bunch, strong man of Shannon County, Missouri; Gopher Bill, pioneer; Allan Bradley, giant of Hedgehog Harbor, Wisconsin; Solomon Shell, Ken-

The Paul Bunyan trademark (far left) of the Red River Lumber Company, designed by W. B. Laughead in 1922. (Left) Paul in 1924, from an illustration by Laughead.

tucky mountaineer; and others. All possessed the unparalleled strength and capacity of Paul Bunyan, their feats often approaching the miraculous. Most also had animals capable of achievements to rival those of Bunyan's ox Babe or his cow Lucy, who ate spruce and balsam boughs to produce milk that Bunyan's loggers could use for cough syrup, saving them

"from many an attack of pneumonia."

The ballyhoo of giants is still very much alive in America. Pressed into community service by journalists and local promoters, these larger-than-life figures beckon to an eager and receptive public, attempting to attract tourist curiosity and dollars, not unlike their role in the Barnum era of petrified men.

The kind of Mules we raise.
Copyright by Martin Post Card Co. 1908.

16

POST CARD

Taking our Geese to market.

Copyright 1909 by Martin Post Card Co.

King Photo

COPYRIGHT 1908
BY ARCHER KING.

A CAPTIVE SPECIMEN

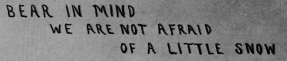

Specimens of our Wool Producers.

Copyright 1910 by
Martin Post Card Co.

Photo by
Tinsley

PRODUCT OF N. DAKOTA.
4 YEARS OLD.
HEIGHT 6 FT 8 INCHES
LENGTH 17 FT.
WEIGHT 4120 LBS.
EXHIBITED BY
L. A. MARSH,
BLISSFIELD, MICH.

20

Feeding time.

Copyright 1909 by Martin Post Card Co.

21

Ol' you Mr. Bull-frog.

Copyright 1910 by Martin Post Card Co.

Angling for Bull-Frogs.

Copyright 1910 by Martin Post Card Co.

I am starting a
brewery and I am
going to use the hops
on the other side.

HOMEGROWN

WHIMSY

When the American frontier had officially vanished in 1890 (according to the census), the hinterlands were open to mass homesteading. Americans fully understood the economic importance of the land west of the Mississippi River, and eager businessmen put forth their best efforts to promote land sales and settlement.

Advertisements for western lands often played with the concept of space and scale. Dakota lands were described as having the "best of the deep rich soil of the valley," and with "excellent water supply." Settlers were thus urged to be smart, act quickly, and get the best. On one of their advertising postcards, The Chase Land Company of South Dakota described Montana as "the State of 'Big Things.'" But no place then was too big, nothing was too great, no land was too rich for the promoters. The weather was always good, and the crops always sprang up overnight. The soil was so fertile that even a footprint would grow. To pick the corn a ten-foot ladder was needed, and, of course, all land was advertised as being next door to the biggest markets in the country, where crops sell easily and at top prices. In a land of such excessive abundance, the fish could never top the lies for size.

Roderick Nash stated in his classic study on wilderness and the American mind that in the most desirable of worlds nature was ordered in the interests of man. Land, therefore, was ideally "flat, fertile and well-watered."

HOW'S THIS
FOR CABBAGE?
SERIES C. No 3.
COPYRIGHT 1909
PHOTO ART SHOP

And so, in such a beneficent natural setting, living could only be effortless and easy. One had but to toss the seed into the field and, zap, a tall, healthy crop would appear.

Would that this were so! In reality, life on the prairie and on the plains was quite often just the opposite—inhospitable, threatening, and fraught with menacing possibilities. It could be so hot one day that the corn popped and so cold the next that a pitcher of water froze so fast that its ice was still warm.

Several well known farmers in this vicinity are in a very serious position, having carelessly become tangled in the rapidly growing corn.

The "NEW HOME" IN THE FAR WEST.

W J Morgan & Co Lith. Cleveland,O.

NEW HOME SEWING MACHINE CC
30 UNION SQUARE N.Y. & ORANGE MASS

Copyrighted A.D.1881.

Between 1870 and 1880, the population of Kansas, Nebraska, and Colorado had increased more than twofold. During the early 1880s, settlement was almost equally rapid in the Dakotas and Rocky Mountain states. Then in the 1880s and 1890s, severe drought and dust storms began to hit some of these areas, frustrating even the most hearty inhabitants. Prices for crops such as corn were so low that farmers burned it for fuel rather than sell it on the open market. No matter what the advertisements promised, life was neither peaceful nor prosperous.

In spite of the physical and economic adversities (or maybe because of them), a unique brand of American folk humor was emerging. Mark Twain expressed it well. "The secret source of humor itself is not

Crateing Immense Strawberries.

WHOLESALE FRUITS

HEWITT-EVANS FRUIT CO.

Copyright 1910 by Martin Post Card Co.

28

Copyright 1909 by Marlin Post Card Co.

Shipping a few of our Peaches.

BAGGAGE

WELLS FARGO

Copyright 1909 by
Marlin Post Card Co.

WELLS FARGO

Harvesting Wheat
Copyright 1908 by Martin Post Card Co.

SCREENING ONIONS THAT ALL
A LARGE BUISNESS ON
A SMALL SCALE

#138 MONEY GROWS ON TREES IN THIS COUNTRY
COPYRIGHT
BY WM. REID
1915

31

joy but sorrow." Often, indeed, it is not prosperity and plenty that generate laughter but hardship; and on the American frontier, there was hardship aplenty. According to Roger Welsch, folklorist of the Plains, "Even today there is a certain pride enjoyed by those who have attained some goal by conquering hardship or surviving a disaster, and, conversely, there is disdain for those who coast along on the bounty of the rich land or a kind providence. So the homesteader magnified the perversity of his chosen land to magnify his own achievement in overcoming those hardships, and he converted the agony to humor in order to make the actual burden seem lighter." The tall tale, therefore, became a tool to help the settler cope with the daily problems of life.

This way of coping became the all-American approach to hard times. Anyone could make a rich countryside lush, but it would take a special ingenuity to make a desert bloom. Often the humor is tongue-in-cheek, with only a hint at the point of it all. Its vision is outrageous and overwhelming, filled with the paradox of reality's being very different from expectation. Delivered deadpan, facetiousness is carried to the extreme. Fantasy and reality are blurred, and there is a fine line to be walked between the credible and the incredible. It's like boasting of making a small fortune—when you started with a big one. Akin to the rural tradition of the liars' bench, or the gathering of local storytellers, the art of the tall tale thrives on competition. Even today in small-town cafés the tables are for bragging, where every farmer has bigger yields than his neighbor no matter what he's got in the bank. Take, for example, the retort of Dr. Binninger as he and some friends were inspecting crops in New Jersey (from an 1896 *Book of Lies*):

Oh, this is very well; very well, indeed, for Jersey. But nothing to what I have seen. In Gastley County, Missouri, I once saw the corn growing to such an unprecedented height, and the stalks so exceptionally vigorous, that nearly every farmer stacked up, for winter firewood, great heaps of cornstalks, cut into cordwood length by power saws run by threshing engines. Matter of fact, one man, Barney Gregory by name, took advantage of the season to win a fortune by preparing cornstalks for use as telegraph poles.

Born with the impulse to tell a story, man has long been fascinated with narration in all its guises. Storytelling and yarn-spinning have adapted to all local and social climates.

To raise this corn see directions other side
Copyright 1909 by Martin Post Card Co.

Some million Eh! Pin

KERRVILLE

Grown by Frank Boulls, near Jennings, Ks.

Kansas Pumpkin.

Photo by Floyd Horton, Kan.

CROP OF 1909 RAISED AT RIPON WIS.

ONIONS

COPR. BY ALFRED STANLEY JOHNSON JR OCT 20 1909 WAUPUN WIS.

Here is the place we grow large cabbage

We raise tons of Sweetpotatoes.

Copyright 1909 by Martin Post Card Co.

36

The best half dozen in
Michigan. Planted
with a "Keystone"
Potato Planter.
Manufactured by -
    A. J. PLATT,

        STERLING, ILL.

Pumpkins grown on our soil
are profitable.

A Scene at a Logging Camp.

Copyright, 1911, by R.F. Brown.

A Souvenir from Rib Lake, Wis.

The tall tale's origin is difficult to trace, but according to Carol Brown this form of humor has been around a very long time. Plutarch (c. A.D. 46–120) recorded a tale about words that froze and could not be heard until they were thawed.

> *Antiphanes said humorously that in a certain city words congealed with the cold the moment they were spoken, and later, as they thawed out, people heard in the summer what they had said to one another in the winter.*

This tale appeared again in Castiglione's *Book of the Courtier* (1528) when a character reported a story, "affirmed as positive fact," of how merchants screamed across a frozen river, unable to hear one another. Finally some local people who had seen this happen before, built a fire on the river's ice and thawed out the words.

This same concept was repeated hundreds of years later when a story in the *Nebraska Farmer* of 1925 related how a J. O. Lobb noticed "his brother's words freezing . . . , caught some of them in a sack, and carried them home and thawed them out by the fire." How cold was it?—so cold that people had to dig down twenty feet into the ground just to read the thermometer; so cold that the fire froze on the candles and they had to be buried to make it dark enough for sleeping.

According to Linda Dégh, folklorist and professor at Indiana University, what she calls "Tales of Lying" can be analyzed.

FISHING FOR BEAVER TROUT
ICEBERG COVE

MEMPHREMAGOG FUR BEARING TROUT (BEAVER TROUT)
LAKE MEMPHREMAGOG, NEWPORT, VT.

She describes the telling itself as rhythmical and rapid, stressing the virtuoso accumulation of absurdities rather than the content. Outside the realm of either possibility or probability, the world of lies is a world of superfolk who inhabit a land of giant vegetation or preposterous creatures.

The lying tale remains extremely popular all over the world, and even today new variations develop. Besides the usual hunting and fishing stories, unbelievable adventures of soldiers, sailors, travelers, and other sportsmen are common. However, a remarkably different crop developed in the Anglo-American tradition of the New World. Its fruit, the tall tale, is a continually reinterpreted idea that has long been popular in America, particularly in the Midwest.

The yarn is something else. Long, rambling, extravagant, its purpose is to accumulate a certain kind of detail in order to produce an effect. The tall tale moves more quickly to reach its goal. Carol Brown describes the tall tale as a fictional narrative told as fiction. Often it masquerades as a true narrative when it is related as a personal report or an anecdote. Sometimes the tall tale is interpreted as truth both by design of the narrator and by listeners who act as though they believe it to be true.

Benjamin A. Botkin, editor of *A Treasury of American Folklore*, explains that tall tales originate when the delicate balance between truth and untruth is tilted in favor of the latter. Improving on actual happenings rather than outright lying is one distinguishing feature. He also points out a prevailing interest in freaks of nature whose incongruity proceeds partly from

Jack Rabbits Grow Big In Kansas
Stovall Studio, Dodge City, Kansas Copyrighted 1936

101
WHY BIG GAME HUNTERS LIKE
ALASKA

RABBIT HUNTING AROUND JOHNSONBURG, PA.

PHEASANT HUNTING IN SOUTH DAKOTA

41

"I SAW HIM GO IN HERE"
SERIES C. 44. Copyright 1909 By Oscar Erickson.

POST CARD

Arrowhead Art Shop Newport, Vt.

THE COON THAT WENT A HUNTING—ME.
Series C 32 Copyright 1911 By Photo Art Shop.

BARNES CAMP

541

Nip + Tuck with a Bass.

Copyright 1911 by W. H. Martin.

Landing a good one.

Copyright 1910 by Martin Post Card Co.

The Bass I caught.

Copyright 1909 by W. H. Martin.

LITTLE BUTCH RIDES HIS PET BASS ON GRAND LAKE ©EB-54

I Finally got Him.

Copyright 1910 by Martin Post Card Co.

HICKEN'S FUR BEARING TROUT
Iceberg Lake

Photo by R. E. Marble, Belton, Montana

Fur Herring,
to be found only in
Rice Lake, Wis.

PIPE, FITTINGS & BRASS GOODS.

COPR FEB 1 '10
BY ALFRED STANLEY JOHNSON JR.
WAUPUN WIS.

BIG PIKE

GREAT NORTHERN PICKERAL

THE ONE WE BROUGHT HOME

CAUGHT ON TACKLE BOUGHT AT JOHNSON'S SPORTING GOODS STORE, ORR, MINN.

PREPARING BAIT
FAWCETTS BREEZY POINT LODGE
BIG PELICAN LAKE, PEQUOT, MINN.
PHOTO BY ANDREW

Capture of the Hodag At
Rhinelander, Wis.

the contrast between fact and fancy. Often these tales gain credence because, as first-hand accounts of eyewitnesses or participants, they are backed up with the implied guarantee of "I saw it myself," analogous to the scientific fact that photographs don't lie.

The use of freaks of nature for tall-tale material is associated with the American habit of boosting, or boasting, and with the pioneer trait of "laughing it off" or making light of misfortunes. Everett Dick, in *The Sod-House Frontier*, described how an Englishman in 1870 was dumbfounded by the pioneers' tendency to exaggerate, or as he put it, "to gas, boast and blow."

No one saw any harm in telling a "whopper"; that is, a lie that no one would believe. Many, he observed,

JACKALOPE (RABBIT WITH HORNS)

Osborn
X-1732

would have felt it not worth while to speak if they could not stretch the truth a bit. There was little difference, the observer found, between one thousand and ten thousand to the Westerner. A few dozen snakes would as readily be called one as the other. A few more flies than were agreeable would be called "wagon loads." The visitor concluded with the observation that the pioneers had a light lively way of speaking and that they delighted in dry jokes.

Botkin described this "product of the untrammeled imagination" as an "other-world" that bears a faint resemblance and a direct relation to the heaven on earth described in early Western guidebooks and land advertisements—"out of whose boasts of marvels of climate and soil many whoppers have sprung." In a land where distances and natural resources could be endless, both geography and human enterprises were on a grand scale, with the boundary between fact and fantasy hard to distinguish. The Idaho potato story recorded in *Idaho Lore*, which was prepared by the Federal Writers' Project of the Works Progress Administration in 1939, promotes just this image:

> In the Snake River Valley lives an old-timer who is known as Old Jim. Old Jim comes to town now and then and boasts of the fertility of his land, but complains that he is unable to market the stuff. He grew pumpkins, but they were so large he could not get them onto a wagon, and then ventured into potatoes.

Nellie. Does papa raise any
potatoes like these, that only
Take twelve for a load?
I want to see you dear. With
lots of love from
Grandma Tuell.

Caribou. Maine. Potatoes.

Miss Nellie Tuell
Princeton.
Mamie.

VICTOR

TANEY. CO. SWEET
POTATO.

McKINNEY PHOTO
HOLLISTER
MO.

Oh you Spud!

BAN GOR & AROOS TOOK 6742

Nebraska Potatoes

Copyright 1905,
By S.D. Butcher &
Son.
Kearney, Neb.

A CARLOAD OF JUNCTION CITY POTATOES

Photograph by E.J. Kuhn.

POTATO
FROM MERCER COUNTY MO.

SHELTON
BROS

When, two years ago, a CCC camp was established nearby, Old Jim was approached by a man who wanted to buy a hundred pounds of spuds.

"Only a hundred pounds?" he asked, scratching his pate. "No, I can't do it. I wouldn't cut a spud in two for no one."

SELLING
THE AMERICAN DREAM

E very possible medium in popular culture helped to spread exaggerative humor. One early visual prototype of tall-tale comedy came from the settlers' heartfelt response to the bounty of their homesteads at the turn of the century. With unbridled fervor, people contributed time and energy to local agricultural festivals and celebrations. In the Midwest, corn was over and over again a favorite theme.

In 1887 the Sioux City, Iowa, city fathers came up with a novel idea to express gratitude for a decade of great agricultural prosperity and to create goodwill for their city. Why not erect a palace made of corn? As the *Daily Journal* put it, "St. Paul and Montreal can have their ice palaces, which melt at the first approach of spring, but Sioux City is going to build a palace of the product of the soil that is making it the great pork packing center of the Northwest." The idea inspired the city's inhabitants, for they had a keen sense of appreciation for corn's role in their good fortune. "Corn Is King" was the local slogan in an area gone "corn crazy." Long the dominant grain in American agriculture, corn was symbolically the perfect building material for a temple of thanksgiving, an homage to the harvest gods.

Architecturally, the resulting building defied classification; it looked like nothing ever seen before—more Moorish than American. Its 100-foot central tower was adorned with a huge cupola, and the structure was graced with arched windows, minarets, and pinnacles. Flying buttresses

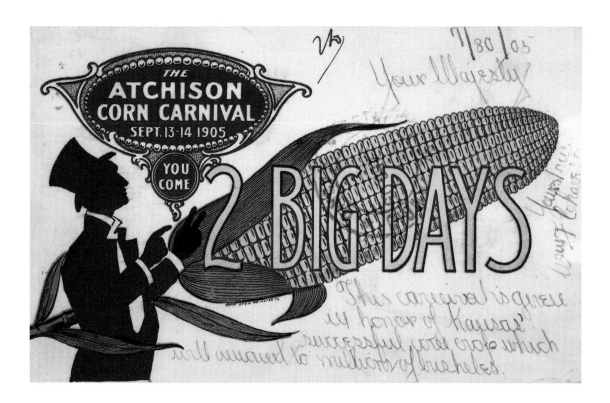

On the preceding page, the fifth and last Sioux City, Iowa, Corn Palace, 1891. Courtesy Iowa State Historical Department, Des Moines, Iowa.

swept gracefully down from the four turrets of the cupola to the corner towers, constituting the most conspicuous feature of the palace, and contributed to an appearance of exaggerated fantasy quite in keeping with the ornate exterior.

Marveling at their prodigious accomplishment in creating the first corn palace, the citizens of Sioux City quickly made plans for a second, then a third, then a fourth, and finally a fifth, the grandest one of all. Its arched facade was covered with red corn, creating an illusion of carved rock. Above the balcony was openwork draped in oats, converging below the broad blue frieze at the base of the great central dome. A triumphant procession of domestic animals was portrayed upon this

belt of blue by the use of dark seeds and grasses. Above the frieze were minarets. Decorated with indigo corn at the base, they passed through nature's spectrum in shades of purple, red, orange, and yellow to dazzling white. The blue and gold capitol of the dome supported a huge yellow cornucopia pouring forth the treasure of the fields.

With the natural demise of this most fabulous palace, the era of the Sioux City Corn Palaces came to a premature end. Although the promoters had fully intended an even more grandiose one for the following year, a ravaging flood caused such a considerable loss of life and property that there was no human energy or resources left for celebration.

"Mrs. Allaman's Pony Feature in Parade," from the program of the Corn Carnival, Atchison, Kansas, 1902.

In 1894 the town of Atchison, Kansas, began its tradition of a Corn Carnival. By 1902, according to a contemporary account, some 30,000 citizens witnessed that year's parade, "the prettiest spectacle the West has ever seen." There were 87 floats and some 13 marching bands taking part in the festivities, which included streets "hedged on every side with tall, plumy corn stalks" and lined with cheering spec-

tators. The Corn Carnival developed in Atchison a religious type of fervor in which pride in the land knew no bounds.

For forty-three-year-old Henry Worrall, an Englishman by birth, Kansas of 1868 was a land of great opportunity. Moving from Cincinnati, Ohio, to Topeka, then a bustling town of about 5,000 people, he became a popular musician. Today, however, he is remembered only for his drawing of

Mrs. Allaman's Pony Feature in Parade.

Grown At SARCOXIE. Mo.

Sprague Studio

Ozark CORN

The "Man with the Hoe" and the corn he grew

GATHERIN' CORN.

Making fuel of the cob.
Copyright 1908 by
Archer King.

King
Photo.

LOADING MAMMOTH CORN, WASH.

King
Photo.

Copyright, 1908,
by Archer King.

Gathering corn in our country.
Copyright 1909 by Martin Post Card Co.

Hawled it by the Dray Load

NEBRASKA CORN.

IOWA CORN.

L. L. Bocher
Cimity
Oregon

CORN IS KING

Copyrighted 190
Bailey Post Card Co
Hutchinson

No 871

Copyright 1907
By The Rotograph Co. N.Y.

CORN AS WE GROW IT IN INDIANA.

The land of Big Corn.

Copyright 1909 by Martin Post Card Co.

WAYNE
SEP
21
6 PM
1910
NEBR.

OKLA. CORN

LACY Photo

CORN CARNIVAL SMITH TRENTON. MO. 1908.

Copyrighted Photograph 1908 by Wm. H. Martin

OUR County Fair Contest on corn.

GOUNTY FAIR.

"Drouthy Kansas," which he produced in response to derogatory characterizations of his new home state by Eastern friends.

Worrall's view of Kansas life took shape in a tall-tale drawing of Kansas as a land of plenty. Huge clusters of grapes hung heavily on their vines; the corn was so gargantuan, it had to be chopped down with a hatchet. A giant tuber was being lifted out of the ground by means of a lever and fulcrum, and one pumpkin was so huge that two men, rather than attempt to move it, were cutting it into pieces with a shovel. Water was in such great supply that it overflowed the riverbanks, and the words "50 to the Acre" indicated the fruitfulness of the adjoining wheat field. This bountiful image became so popular that it soon appeared in many books and periodicals as well as on promotional brochures encouraging settlement in Kansas.

In another effort to match America's greatness with a suitable monument of scale, Gutzon Borglum did what many said couldn't be done. With few precedents to guide him, he carved into South Dakota's Mount Rushmore four giant visages of epic national heroes: George Washington, "father of the nation"; Thomas Jefferson, leader in the growth westward; Theodore Roosevelt, conservationist and expansionist; and Abraham Lincoln, the great emancipator.

Technically, the job was stupefying. Nonetheless, Borglum persevered, and after finally receiving financial support from the Federal government, the sculptor asserted full mastery over the mountain. He redesigned the monument nine times during construction and ultimately intended to carve the presidents to the waist.

DROUTHY KANSAS.

E. SEARS. SC. N.Y.

WELCOME TO THE LAND OF OPPORTUNITIES

OFFICIAL KANSAS DAY POST CARD
PUBLISHED UNDER THE AUSPICES OF
KANSAS DEVELOPMENT ASSOCIATION

KANSAS

POPULATION	1,700,000
AREA	82,158 SQUARE MILES
ACRES IN CULTIVATION	43,000,000
AVG. NO. ACRES PER FARM	244
AVERAGE VALUE PER ACRE	$40
PRODUCTS FOR 1912	$350,000,000
LIVE STOCK	$255,000,000
AVERAGE BU WHEAT	70,000,000
AVERAGE BU CORN	105,000,000

GREATEST ALFALFA LAND IN WORLD
OPPORTUNITIES WORTH MILLIONS
WILL YOU SHARE THEM?

WICHITA. At the junction of the Arkansas and Little Rivers. Population 65,000. Manufacturing and jobbing point and center of rich agricultural section. Distributing point for the Southwest. Annual bank clearings 167 millions. Two packing houses and stockyards. Six trunk line railroads, 54 trains daily. Forty miles interurban service. Forty miles street railway. Wichita wants industries, conventions, more intensive farming.
WICHITA BUSINESS ASSOCIATION

COPYRIGHTED 1912 H. R. SCHMIDT AND CO.

AD ASTRA PER ASPERA

SEWARD

When Borglum died in 1941, the mammoth work was left unfinished, but it has given physical definition to the American dream. Symbolically, the four frontier presidents look out over a vast expanse, perpetually reminding us of America's strength and vitality. We, in turn, gaze at them and are reminded that man sometimes can do what he's told is impossible, that America is a land of impossible dreams come true.

In 1934, *Fortune* magazine published "The Great American Roadside," a report on "the restlessness of the American people"—which the Depression had done little to keep at home. These restless tourists began to be bombarded with all kinds of stimuli: giant billboards, "tea rooms built like teapots," wigwam villages, "stands built like tamales" or "in fact almost any eye-widening outlandishness you can imagine!" Distant relatives of the cigar-store indian and the eighteenth-century oversize trade sign, these structures, in a growing era of the automobile, were intended to slow you down and get your attention. Hopefully, purchases would follow. Accordingly, with its love of the tall tale,

Oil company advertisement in the official program for the unveiling of the Washington head, Mount Rushmore, June 1930. Courtesy Rex Alan Smith.

The CLIMAX OF A DELIGHTFUL MOTOR TRIP

"THE BIG COFFEE POT".

ONE OF THE OLD LAND MARKS, WINSTON-SALEM, N. C.   59029

THE WIGWAMS. FREE MUSEUM, ROUTE 17, JASPER, N.Y.

Miss Minne Sota

Made from S. E. Minnesota grains and grasses in the real estate office of J. L. GRISWOLD, Dodge Center, Minn.

Gould-07

September 30th   - - - -   Texas Rice Day

"GROW RICE FOR WEALTH"
"EAT RICE FOR HEALTH"

Want to know more about it ? --- Ask nearest Railroad Agent, or write

JOS. HELLEN,
G. P. A. - T. & N. O. R. R.

T. J. ANDERSON,
G. P. A. - G. H. & S. A. R. R.

HOUSTON, TEX.

Be sure and secure a copy of our booklets entitled "Texas and Louisiana Rice" and "A Few Things About Rice and how to Cook it."

Our western Queen of Plenty

No.100 1/2

copyrighted 1909
BY Z.D.Butcher&Son.
Kearney Neb.

Fall Opening 1909

Queen of Harvest
J.W.Milliken's Fall Opening

the Midwest embraced these roadside curiosities with gusto. Although they existed (and still exist today) just about everywhere in the Union, a state like Minnesota has hugged them to death.

Karal Ann Marling has written of this in *The Colossus of Roads:*

> *Although colossi advertise festivals, statuary and organized revelry are complementary assertion of local identity. They mark off a stretch of time and a node of place from the continuum of the summertime highways. Colossi locate the edge of town, the route to the business district, its principal attractions. Once over the borderline between movement and stasis, the tourist has effectively left ordinary circumstances behind and is ready for the games, the beauty queens, the costumes, the rituals, and the comestibles with which Americans observe festive occasions.*

As at the Pumpkin Festival in Circleville, Ohio, or the Watermelon Festival in Hope, Arkansas, farmers show off the pick of autumn's harvest and await the judges' pronouncements of "biggest" and "best" quite as eagerly as teenaged beauties anticipate being crowned the next harvest queen; folks come from all over!

The boosterism of showing off the biggest and the best is part of the American vision. Conquering the frontier is what America is all about. And we never stop demonstrating how it can be done.

Carving one of our
WATERMELONS.
Copyright 1909—Martin Post Card Co.

To the "Bunch"

Lindale Station,

Minneapolis,

Minn.

This melon is much
smaller than the average
as the season was very
dry, and melons did not
mature. You ought to see
one in a good season.
Webster City, Iowa.
Oct. 10th. 1914
503, B.

© 1914 F.C. RUEGNITZ

ONE OF THE MELONS
WATER MELON DAY — WEBSTER CITY, IA.

PHOTOGRAPHS

DON'T LIE

Thanks to technological advances in photography, the tall-tale postcard (also called "exaggerated" and "freak") inevitably came into being. It is easy to see a relationship between the tall tale of story form and its pictorial postcard correlative. Both are humorous, created by instinct, and unrelated to any established school. No handbook can detail the techniques necessary for their production. Creativity, cleverness, and often anonymity are basic characteristics of both. Unlike the feckless farmer who ordered a pair of fur-coated chickens out-of-season and found them sweltering to death in the warm weather, the maker of the tall-tale postcard had to carefully devise whimsical combinations that would extend contemporary humor into the visual realm. It was a trial-by-error way of doing things, combining the right image with the right straight line. Basing the impact of their work on the premise that photographs don't lie, these wily creators produced a body of postcards that illustrate American folk humor at its "apple pie" best.

Photography was invented in 1839 and evolved rapidly in a changing economy where an innovative entrepreneur could find unlimited opportunities. In 1888 George Eastman brought out his great invention, the "Kodak," which was a simple box camera that combined the roll-film idea with the plate camera in a compact and easily manipulated form. It took round pictures, 2½ inches in diameter, and came loaded for 100 exposures. When the

Going To Market — From Eugene Or the Exchange

roll was finished, the Kodak camera was returned to the factory for unloading, reloading, and developing the film. The first Kodak camera was not a handy pocket model, but when compared to the complexity of equipment that previously confronted the interested amateur it was a miracle of achievement. Picture-taking had been reduced to the simplicity of the advertising slogan, "You press the button, we do the rest."

By 1902 the Eastman Kodak Company was manufacturing postcard-size photographic paper on which images could be printed directly from negatives. This allowed a business of instant portraits to flourish and launched professional photographers into the pursuit of limited-production postcards. Local scenes, buildings, and events could be inexpensively produced for sale even in small quantities. Between 1906 and 1910, Eastman Kodak further promoted the hobby of amateur postcard photography by offering to print postcards from amateurs' negatives for only a few cents a card.

The postcard, like photography, was a European import. Dr. Emanuel Herrmann, the moving force behind the concept, was an Austrian economics professor, who, in 1869, after analyzing postal revenues and letter-writing habits, concluded that a cheaper, more informal method of communication should be introduced. Soon thereafter, the Austrian prestamped, government-issue "postal card" was made available. These government postals won immediate acceptance; people indeed found them inexpensive and convenient for brief messages. Within a few years, most European countries followed suit and pro-

duced their own postal cards. In 1873 the United States did as well.

Manufactured of stiff paper with a one-cent stamp printed in the upper right-hand corner of its front, the cream-colored American postal card instructed the user to write the address on the right-hand side and the message on the left. The back of the card was completely blank. No variation in size, shape, or color was allowed.

Entrepreneurs on both sides of the Atlantic calculated that with the governmental postals so successful, there surely must be a good market for a different kind of postcard—perhaps one with a picture on the back side. Soon European postcards

REEDLEY PRODUCTION.   REEDLEY LAND CO.

A very fine boy, and very good corn,
Both raised in Kansas, Sure as you'r born.
Come get you a farm out here in the west
Where we raise the crops for a Big Contest.

EASTER GREETINGS.

I COULD TURKEY TROT WITH YOU FOREVER
2160 © Photocraft G.

Copyright Photograph
1909 M W Bailey
Hutchinson Ks

no 870

The Kansas Hen

GOING TO THE Mo. STATE POULTRY SHOW. Smith TRENTON, MO. DEC. 1908.

The Modern Farmer.

Copyright 1909 by Martin Post Card Co.

appeared that pictured tourist attractions such as hotels and restaurants, as well as standardized greetings. Alert photographers jumped on the bandwagon and produced postcards that would earn them extra money during the tourist season. "A Professional," writing in *The British Journal of Photography* in 1903, urged photographers to wake up to new opportunities in the postcard business.

> *The best subjects for regular sale are the stock views of the town, the principal business thoroughfares, public buildings, and chief residential roads. The latter especially are growing in importance as the post-card cult spreads, for people who have met at the holiday resorts and wish to exchange greetings through the post like to have a view of their own road, if such happens to present a good appearance. . . . Local "characters" of the streets, if well known and at all picturesque, are sound subjects, and easily secured with a hand camera.*

Europeans derived great pleasure from the variety of picture postcards, and by the early 1900s collecting them had become a popular hobby. Albums and scrapbooks were compiled in which different postcard collections could be viewed by the entire family. As ubiquitous as the family Bible, these albums included vacation remembrances, portraits, and often exotic views of alien lands and peoples. A fascination with collecting and the need to learn more about the world seemed of paramount importance to this public.

Meanwhile, American interest in the

The Olson Automatic Photograph Printing Machine.

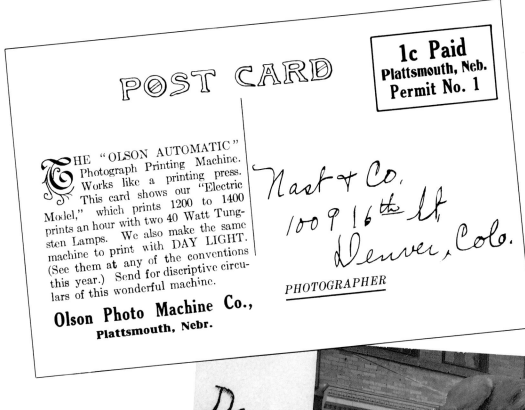

1c Paid
Plattsmouth, Neb.
Permit No. 1

THE "OLSON AUTOMATIC" Photograph Printing Machine. Works like a printing press. This card shows our "Electric Model," which prints 1200 to 1400 prints an hour with two 40 Watt Tungsten Lamps. We also make the same machine to print with DAY LIGHT. (See them at any of the conventions this year.) Send for discriptive circulars of this wonderful machine.

Olson Photo Machine Co.,
Plattsmouth, Nebr.

Nast & Co.
1009 16th St,
Denver, Colo.

PHOTOGRAPHER

Dog on Good Show.

During the Flood on Griswold St.
Great sport for the Boys.
© 1910. Hubel.

Has the D.U.R. Franchise Expired on Griswold?

©1910 Hubel.

3776 NORTH LAND HEADED UP WOODWARD AVE DETROIT

Private Mailing Card

AUTHORIZED BY
ACT OF CONGRESS
MAY 19 1898

62
1121 King Alphonso of Spain,
Madrid,
Spain

98
1091

postcard did not abate. By the 1870s, publishers in the United States had begun printing greetings and advertisements on the backs of government postals. In 1893 privately printed picture postcards came into general use when thousands were sold as souvenirs of the World's Columbian Exposition in Chicago. In 1898 postal regulations granted the same mailing privileges for privately printed cards as for government-issue postals. The inexpensive penny postage fee made it possible for the ordinary person to afford to send postcards and contributed to their popularity, but even more important were developments in the postal system.

Prior to the inception of the Rural Free Delivery system in 1898, home mail delivery had only been available in towns of ten thousand or more inhabitants. Rural residents often had to travel great distances to reach a local post office, and for them receipt of mail was sporadic at best. Although the R.F.D. system took a few years to be completely absorbed into America's fledgling communications system, by 1906 delivery routes had been firmly established. Home mail delivery was now on a daily basis. People felt closer to their neighbors and friends and consequently began to use the mail in ways that had never been contemplated.

When it became possible to reproduce photographs cheaply, newspapers and magazines took rapid advantage. They became less wordy, for journalists began to communicate with pictures. By 1900 the photograph was associated with news, and as such photography began to appear daily in the American household. Periodicals such as *The World's Work* began to specialize in "photo-stories."

When photographic postcards first appeared, postal regulations permitted nothing but the address and stamp on the backs. Any message had to be written on the margins of the photograph. The easing of this restriction in 1907 to allow a message area on the backs led to a substantial growth in photographic postals.

Like the printed word, the photograph took on an inherent air of authority. It recorded facts, captured a "real" likeness of a person, and illustrated technological advances. It gave instant visual access to the past, being called upon to furnish a "true" picture of events, places, and things. Consequently, as Paul Fussell explained in *Abroad*, because tall-tale postcards were "photographed" their comedy intensified, "parodying the more sober traveler's assumption that he may not be believed without bringing home photographic evidence."

LIVING
LIVING

IN THE GOLDEN AGE

Who were these purveyors of hard-core photographic evidence? In the early 1900s, photography was not a lucrative profession, so most photographers were forced to hold other jobs. Since their finances were often tied directly to the fortunes of their communities, needless to say their economic base was precarious. If crops did well, their neighbors had money for "extras"; if the weather was bad and crop prices were down, little could be done to promote interest in something as frivolous as a photograph.

Often local photographers sought contract work for the government or the railroads as alternate ways to make a living. When railroads opened new vistas, they took photographers with them to record both acreage and construction. Huge grants of government land earlier given to the railroads for right-of-way were sold off in small parcels at low prices. This land, powerful symbol that it was, became the stuff to dream of. Seductive advertising by both the government and the railroads drew settlers westward, offering them a promised land of plenty. To set out for a distant territory where an apple had to be fetched in a wheelbarrow, cornstalks were solid enough for railroad ties, and a silver dollar when planted could become a crop of eagles, one would have to put believing before seeing. But a small group of individualistic photographers, most of them living at the geographic crossroads of the Midwest, helped disappointed settlers cope with the sometimes

WHY INVEST IN KANSAS PACIFIC
LANDS?

Because you have the vast expanse of 5,000,000 Acres to select from, with every variety of Land, Bottom and Upland, Undulating Valley, and Rolling Prairie.

Because the PURITY of the CLIMATE is UNSURPASSED—long Summers, short Winters, and genial skies.

Because the fertility of the soil *can't be beaten.* Where else can be found a soil of such rich, dark loam, varying from 3 to 15 feet in depth?

Because in proof of this, the unprecedented Crops proclaim Kansas to be the *Banner Wheat and Corn State of the Union.*

Because its Rivers, Streams and Creeks abound in every County along the Road.

Because Springs of purest water are to be found in every section.

Because of the vastness of its water power for manufacturing purposes.

Because for Stock Raising and Wool Growing, the nutritious character of its wide grassy ranges has been proved invaluable.

Because all the Lands are within an easy distance of the Great Iron Thoroughfare of the West.

Because Towns and Cities are rapidly springing up all along its entire length, with all their attendant advantages.

Because wherever a setttlement is formed, the moral and religious well being of its inhabitants are duly cared for.

Last but not least.

Because the Prices are *very low.*

Because the Terms of Credit are long, easy, liberal, and within the reach of all.

Because if you buy 160 Acres, your ride out to seek Lands will be free.

WHEN TO COME? AT ONCE!

The Company are more desirous to get their Lands settled up and improved, thereby increasing the business of its Railroad, than they are to hold them with the view of realizing higher prices, the prosperity of the settlers being the prosperity of the Railroad.

Archer King

inhospitable acres through their giant sense of humor and intense commitment to their newfound land.

Archer King was such a man. He is remembered in his native Table Rock, Nebraska, as a debonair lover of automobiles who enjoyed giving neighbors rides in his own homemade vehicles. Constructing four of them from scratch, he utilized sundry miscellaneous parts from household utilities such as a "baby carriage, gasoline torch, base threshing machine, corn planter and telephone instrument." To make a living, he ran picture shows in many of the small towns in southeastern Nebraska and also worked in his wife's family nursery business.

As a photographer, he operated in Table Rock and then in a photography studio in the nearby town of Shubert, where he created an assortment of exaggerated images by skillfully combining two images into one—a "montage." Original pasteups exist that demonstrate his detailed composites. In "Too much for the elevator," local townspeople lend an additional bit to an inside joke. In another, two pretty women chop kernels off an immense corncob only to have them pop in the hot weather. "Leap Year is gone, it's your turn to pop," says the legend.

Walter T. Oxley was another talented amateur who became a professional photographer. Born in 1872 in Britt, Iowa, he attended rural schools and spent one term at the Northern Iowa Normal College. In 1896 he married and subsequently went to live on a farm at Foxhome, Minnesota. Several years later, to pursue his interest in photography, he sold this property and moved to Fergus Falls, Minnesota, where he worked for the Carlson Studio prior to opening his own photo-finishing business.

Intensely committed to his community, Oxley had the distinction of drawing up the local petition for the first mail route in Wilkin County, and shortly thereafter he conceived the idea of the Rural Farmers Telephone Service. Always inventing, he patented such items as a postcard printer (later sold to Eastman Kodak), a grain-sack tie, and a whistling signal for a gasoline pump—clearly a device ahead of its time.

Commercial work was the studio specialty, but Oxley, doing what many a rural photographer of his era had to do, photographed school classes, disasters, accidents, post-mortems, and funeral group portraits. In addition, he took part in the westward expansion in 1908 when the Columbia Company hired him to go to Oregon and photograph their property for advertising postcards. Later, in 1916, he photographed Texas acreage for another land company. Oxley loved to tell the story of how he kept ahead of the game by quickly printing pictures from wet negatives in the men's room as the train traveled to its next stop. When local people wanted to know what the land looked like at the previous stop, Oxley was able to produce photographic evidence.

Ever resourceful, he also produced postcards of local interest. Some were simple frontal views of buildings in and around Fergus Falls; others recorded exceptional events such as a flood, cyclone, or train wreck. By producing such cards, Oxley helped to document the growth of an American community.

Also known as a storyteller and a bit

SOME TIMES WE GET A BIG ONE

Walter T. Oxley, self-portrait with one that didn't get away.

of a jokester, Oxley loved a good yarn. Hunting and fishing were two favorite hobbies, so it is no surprise that many of his postcards were based on these themes.

Unlike Oxley, *Alfred Stanley Johnson* was brought up in the photography business. Born to Alfred and Elizabeth in 1863 in Waupun, Wisconsin, he first learned photography from his father, who as early as 1868 was advertising himself as "proprieter of Johnson's Gallery." From 1875 to 1878, *The Waupun Leader News* announced, "All kinds of sun pictures taken. Enameled, cameo, and souvenirs crayon, India ink, oil and watercolors. Permanent photographs by a new process." A year later the *News* told of "artist Johnson making the new carbon picture—something eminently ahead of the ordinary photograph."

By 1891, son Stanley (also Alfred Stanley but not called Alfred because of his father) had opened his own gallery. Years later a newspaper account stated that he "has issued some neat views of the prison [Wisconsin State Prison, located in Waupun] on post cards and is making a hit with them especially in the neighboring towns."

Known for innovation, Johnson produced "photo jewelry" in 1902 and was granted a patent for a device to wash photographic prints in 1907. Also in that year, he photographed residences as well as streets and buildings in Waupun, making them into souvenir postcards to sell at the news depot in the local post office. His exaggerated postcards, the majority created from 1909 to 1913, demonstrate an artistic excellence, complex action, and humorous use of understatement and pun.

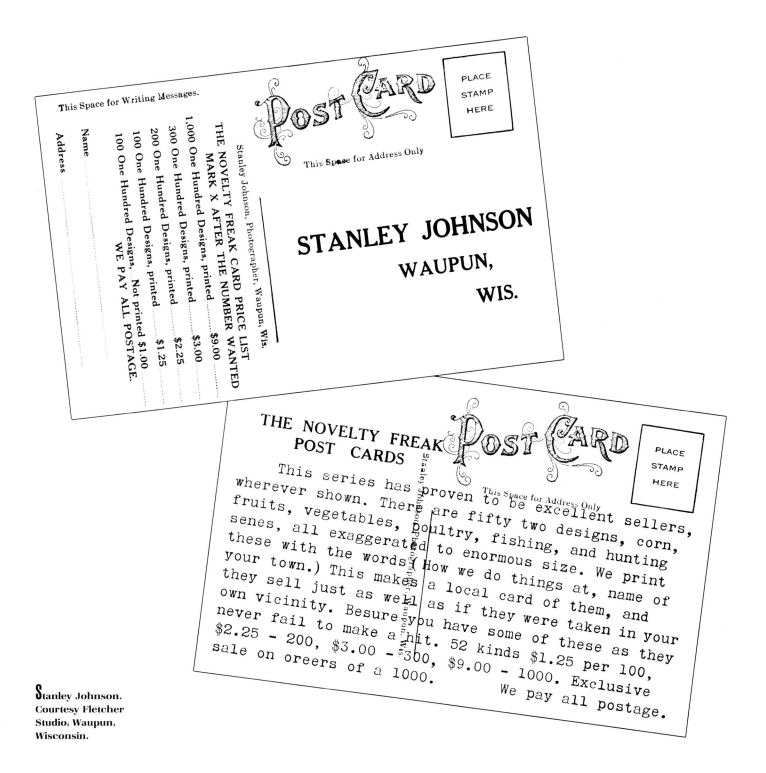

Stanley Johnson.
Courtesy Fletcher
Studio, Waupun,
Wisconsin.

To arrive at his finished product, Johnson carefully prepared two or three photographs to use in his montage. The first was a shot of the background scenery with real people (usually children) holding props and poised in their staged positions for the imagined composite image. The second and third pictures were close-ups of the focal object, often a vegetable, fruit, fish, or animal. Johnson would then cut out the enlarged figure and paste it delicately onto the background scene. His precise cutting and pasting lent an aura of believability to the final image—which he then rephotographed.

Johnson's use of children also helped sustain the appearance of truth in his cards. In "Melon Party," the shape of a watermelon slice cut to size from stiff material is carefully held by his young models. To their left, a boy stands with a hand resting on a prop and his arm upraised, which Johnson later dovetailed exactly with a pasteup photograph of a gigantic melon. The laconic caption expresses wry commentary on the photograph's action.

On the West coast, in California, tourism was creating a great demand for souvenirs, and *Edward H. Mitchell* of San Francisco was filling the need by marketing a series of ten or twelve cards in folders that could be sent as a unit or individually. Although plentiful and dating from 1909 to 1910, these cards are generally static in composition, with little variation or perspective. Basically, they illustrate only a carload of a few nuts, fruits, or vegetables on a flat railroad car. This did not, however, diminish the popularity of these cards. Thousands were sold. But for today's collector, they result in none of the

visual excitement that the work of *William H. Martin* evokes.

"Dad" Martin of Ottawa, Kansas, produced the quintessential exaggerated postcard. Making use of myriad subjects, his work—the best and most varied in the genre—displays a sense of action notably absent in others.

At age twenty-one, he moved to Ottawa from Maple City to learn photography from E. H. Corwin; in 1894 he bought out Corwin's studio. Here he advertised a facility for all types of photography, including portraits and "a specialty made of carbon prints and college groups."

By 1908 Martin was experimenting with "trick photography" postcards, selling the results throughout the nation. These cards with their visually powerful images were so successful that he sold the photography studio in 1909 to turn full attention to the Martin Post Card Company, which an article in *The Evening Herald* of May 24, 1909, announced "turns out 10,000 cards daily." By May of the next year, the local newspaper described the total output of the Martin factory as seven million cards. "Seven times as much photo materials, including plates, paper and chemicals are used by the Martin Company than any other company in the world."

An exaggeration? Maybe. Nonetheless, Martin had made a successful business out of the tall-tale postcard. In Martin's cards, an ear of corn is so huge that a saw must be used to cut it up for fuel. Canning

ILISHED BY CARDINELL-VINCENT CO., OAKLAND, CALIFORNIA

OVERGROWN POTATO FROM CALIFORNIA

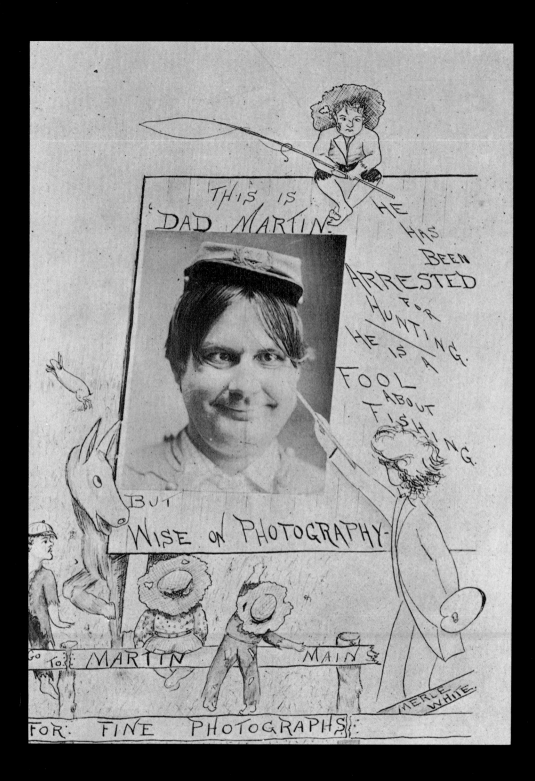

William H. Martin, full-length and portrait made for advertising.

peaches is hard work for some six men who need heavy equipment to accomplish the task. A giant rabbit bounds away as energetic men attempt to capture it. Pumpkins don't just grow; they erupt, lifting houses from their very foundations. And, a watermelon is no longer something to consume but a dwelling for an entire family.

When a swarm of grasshoppers descended on Garden City, Kansas, in 1935, *Frank D. "Pop" Conard*, photographer and owner of a local radio station, didn't leave

Peach Canning Time - on the farm.

Copyright 1910 by Martin Post Card Co.

Copyright 1909 by W.H. Martin

When we go after anything we get it.

Does this remind you of the way we hunted rabbits last winter?

A Pumpkin of "Powerful" growth.

Copyright 1909 by Martin Post Card Co.

114

A Unique Bungalow.

Copyright 1909 by Martin Post Card Co.

town—he went to bed. "At 3:00 A.M.," he later recalled, "all I could think about was grasshoppers." By morning he knew how he could concoct some fun out of this disaster. He took pictures and montaged the grasshoppers with humans. "I didn't do it for adverse impressions of Kansas, but as an exaggerated joke. I made four different cards and distributed them in town. They sold like hotcakes." Conard's postcard business flourished as his stock photographs of grasshoppers and jackrabbits were augmented to include stuffed animals and human models. Relatives and neighbors were continually finding themselves included in these comic composites. Postcards were not a new business endeavor; Conard had been producing them since the 1920s—mainly of dust storms, parades, and social scenes—but his "hopper whoppers" took off like nothing else he had ever done. A master retoucher, Conard often helped out reality by removing blemishes from a face or even by substituting one individual's head for that of another. The joke was never quite over.

Mrs. Euna Olsen, who worked for Conard from 1928 to 1945, estimated in a newspaper interview that she alone printed nearly two million cards

"IN THIS WHEAT BY AND BY."

> It was an original idea. I can tell you he didn't get it from anywhere else. He was a very original man. He always had original ideas. . . . We started out first on dust storms. Then times got, real, real hard. Mr. Conard was very efficient in composing pictures so we went out and caught grasshoppers and took pictures of grasshoppers and trains and stuffed jackrabbits.

Working for one dollar a day, Mrs. Olsen printed the postcards. Six to eight traveling salesmen then called on service stations, cabin camps, and tourist shops to display the cards. In return for selling the nickel cards, dealers received 2½ cents for each. It has been reported that Conard printed some three million cards in all, continuing to market them until his retirement in 1963.

"Haulin Em Out"

#27
CONARD
G.C. K8.

CAPTUREING "WHOPPER HOPPER" NEAR MITCHELL S.D.
THE LARGEST GRASSHOPPER IN EXISTENCE
54 INCHES LONG - WEIGHT 73 POUNDS - HERSEY PHOTO SERVICE

We raise 'em big and ride 'em straight up.

miller studio pix, Pierre, So. Dak.

ROSEBUD PHOTO GREGORY

119

THE TRAIN HOLD-UP

PHOTO BY
F.D. CONARD
No. 43

TELL IT TO THE JUDGE

#25
CONARD
G.C. KS.

"AFTER THE BATTLE"

PHOTO. BY
F.D.CONARD
No. 56.

"MAY THE BEST MAN WIN."
#52-© 1937- F.D.CONARD, GARDEN CITY, KANS.

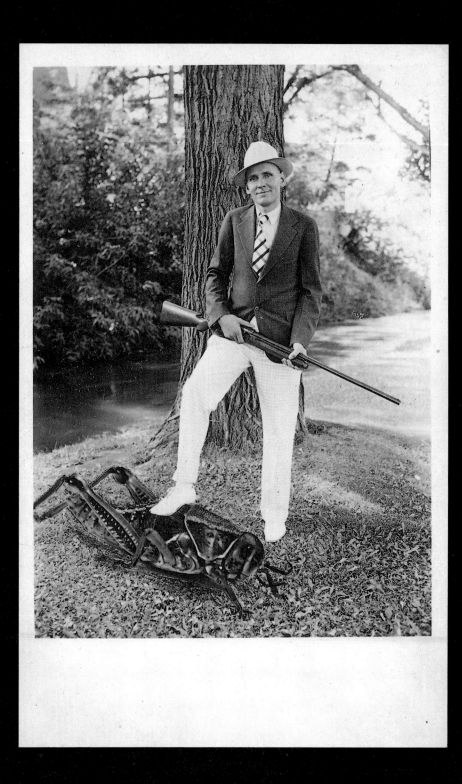

YORNHOLT DRUG STORE

COLE'S STUDIO
GLASGOW MONT.

GRASSHOPPER SHOT NEAR
FORT PECK DAM.

123

IN KANSAS – YOU MAY FISH WHERE YOU PLEASE – THIS PICTURE
IS NOT SPONSERED BY THE C of C   PHOTO – J.B. MUECKE
5/53 OTTAWA – KANS

Following in Conard's footsteps was *Joseph B. Muecke* (later changed to *Mickey*). Born in 1902 he was a professional electrical contractor until moving in 1940 to Ottawa, Kansas, former home of William H. Martin. There he established the Ottawa Engraving Company and also worked as a free-lance photographer. The *Ottawa Herald* depicted him as a "familiar sight in this area, often seen with his big, heavy, 4 × 5 Graphex camera." A lean, sharp-featured man, he had "a delightful sense of humor" and was "a real Ottawa booster." In 1951 he published *Disaster*, a picture story of the great Ottawa flood, and later *Disaster of May 20, 1957*, another picture story, but this time of a tornado. In 1963 he issued *The Thrilling Story of the Waynoka, Oklahoma, Rattlesnake Hunts*, because "every American should know about it just in case the Communists try to invent it."

GETTING
THE MESSAGE ACROSS

Conquering the American frontier took a special brand of courage. The people who had invested their lives in such an enterprise developed a toughness that gave them the ability to laugh in the face of adversity. Their basic attitude was to spread the good news; let no one know the bad. They would widely broadcast any record-smashing crop totals, but keep the knowledge of any disheartening figures from inhabitants of other states.

Living on the Great Plains required a state of mind that demanded a resilient approach toward life. After the Civil War, there were financial panics, droughts, and grasshoppers. An 1874 newspaper reported, "The grasshoppers reappeared here in swarms on Wednesday. The object of their visit is not known, as there is nothing here to eat."

When the corn crop of 1877 was so poor in Saline County, Kansas, that farmers had to send for seed corn before the next crop could be attempted, a newspaper account told of the "owners of corn-shellers in Kansas, this year, complaining that their machines are useless because the ears of corn are so big they cannot get them into the machines."

Whatever may have been the truth about the harvest of salable grain, the yield of tall stories was always bumper. As usual in times of adversity, the local papers were contradictory in their condition reports, boasting of every good field and putting the most hopeful appearance on a bad situa-

The Prosperity of Farmer John in Nebr. 6,000 Bushels

tion. "Wheat crops chuckling all over with laughter and bouyant with hope," wrote one editor, whereas the reality was of drought, wind, chinch bugs, and heat. The spirit of boom optimism did not permit candor, and anyone making a low estimate or a pessimistic prediction was almost certain to be branded a liar.

The frontiersmen's traditional answer to hard times was humor. In the face of scorching summer, cold winter, drought, grasshoppers, and high interest rates, families could only hang in there. When the land dried up, the Plains farmer could still laugh about the report that toll bridge collectors were going broke because cattlemen drove their animals across the dry rivers.

But the land of promise could also be a land of unexplained miracles. Where drought once ruled, now mildew took over. Western Kansas, formerly a scorched desert, became too wet for cattle to range. Boom times were followed by desolate, parched years, causing markets and lives to fluctuate wildly. Desperately, farmers looked back over their shoulders, for there was no place to move on to. The frontier had closed; there was nothing ahead. They now wondered whether they should have so eagerly believed all those stories they read—all that railroad promotion telling of bumper crops, big fortunes made overnight, farms that grew larger and larger with each telling, where a man could start out in the spring and plow a straight furrow until fall, then turn around and harvest back.

The bonanza farms of northern Dakota, a new style of frontier agriculture, had been hyped until they became the

source of many legends. Local newspapers gave the impression that every other farm was a bonanza; they wanted everyone to believe that the Red River was the "Nile of America" and that every settler had made a fortune. Because of these stories, the "boomer" psychology brought in even more newcomers. This is what dreams were made of.

As part of the Northern Pacific's pro-

It MEANS PROSPERITY!

COLORADO
$1,00,000,000.00
FARM CROP
AUTO
1910 — MODEL
OATS
ALFALFA
BARLEY
WHEAT
SPUDS

POST CARD

U.S. POSTAGE

BURROAK,
NOV
24
P.M.
1909

AN INVITATION

COME to Southeast Texas where roses bloom and
grass is green throughout the year, where the
garden furnishes fresh fruits and vegetables every
month. Where all kinds of crops grow quickly, bear
heavily, and bring top prices. Where the summers are
pleasant and the winters ideal. Where the soil is fertile,
the water excellent, the rainfall ample (36 to 48 inches)
and where the Farmer or Investor can treble his money
quicker than anywhere else in the world. For par-
ticulars, address   THE PROVIDENT LAND CO.,
                                               Kansas City, Mo.
Northwest Corner Ninth
and Walnut Streets

Geo. Tren,
Burroak,
Nebr.

There will be many more crops of Pigs but never again a

Crop of Land

Get a slice of the earth while prices are still within your reach. Write to us for a list of our South Dakota land bargains.

Watters Land Agency
G. M. Watters, Mgr., Redfield, S. D.

Northwestern Land Products Show
(TWIN CITY LAND SHOW)

NORTHERN PACIFIC YELLOWSTONE PARK LINE

St. Paul Auditorium - Dec. 12-23, 1911

Here is where the Northwest: }
Minnesota, North Dakota, South Dakota,
Montana, Idaho, Washington, Oregon, Alaska

Will Show You what it can produce and why you should live in this LAND OF FORTUNE. ¶Of course you will come!

motional scheme to attract settlers to the region, this publicity succeeded beyond the dreams of its creators. It not only attracted settlers but also created a lasting impression in people who felt they were victims of a giant hoax. With bitterness they remembered the promises made to them before their arrival. Indeed, the tall-tale postcard reflects the very irony of life on the frontier. Its settlers could be starved, frozen, and then roasted, but you couldn't kill them off. In a land where fortune could take a dramatic turn in an instant, man had to adjust to the likelihood of sudden change, and his ability to deal with it and wear a smile became the American way.

Tall-tale photographers, with their fresh approaches and strong impact, had their own unique styles of homegrown whimsy, and they perpetuated a folk tradition whose origin is deeply rooted in the American dream. Messages on the backs of tall-tale postcards, like immigrant letters home, reveal the heart and spirit of the people.

Under the implicit belief that the camera doesn't lie, reality was fused with illusion for just the briefest of moments—a magic stopping place in time where artful fraud endured. Creating good times to reduce the hardship of reality, turning pain into humor, these larger-than-life visions today delight us with their original and timeless amusement.

BIBLIOGRAPHY

Jay, Robert. *The Trade Card in Nineteenth-Century America.* Columbia: University of Missouri Press, 1987.

Marling, Karal Ann. *The Colossus of Roads.* Minneapolis: University of Minnesota Press, 1984.

Morgan, Hal. *Big Time/American Tall-Tale Postcards.* New York: St. Martin's Press, 1981.

Welsch, Roger L. *Tall-Tale Postcards/A Pictorial History.* New Jersey: A. S. Barnes and Co., 1976.

ACKNOWLEDGMENTS

The authors are deeply indebted to a large number of real-photo postcard collectors, dealers, and other friends who provided information and material for Morgan's collection. Hal Ottaway was the first, and also first to suggest a book.

Timothy Baum, Ove Braskerud, Andreas Brown, Mike Johnston, John and Sandy Millns, Susan Nicholson, Bert Phillips, Don and Newly Preziosi, Hal Ross, Jack and Vicki Stock, Frances Storey, Roger Welsch, and Frank Wood have been essential to putting the necessary information and collection together.

Lucille Williams, Morgan's mother, did extensive research on W. H. Martin, and William "Bill" Martin and Ross Martin were especially helpful.

Information was also provided by the Waupun Historical Society, Finney County Historical Society, Mildred M. Rintoul, Lloyd Oxley, Laura Turnbull, Plattsmouth Historical Society, and Esther Bemmels.

Morgan is particularly grateful to his wife, Lynda, and his children, Jon, Daren, Denise, and Evan, for their support, cooperation, and understanding.

We especially wish to thank Walton Rawls and Julie Rauer of Abbeville for their good ideas and patience during the several months it took to put the book together. The authors also give special thanks to each other; the book was a good team effort.

THE KIND OF CORN WE RAISE AT OGDEN,